From Reading to Writing

O. M. Thomson

Oxford University Press 1980

Oxford University Press, Walton Street, Oxford OX2 6DP

Oxford London Glasgow
New York Toronto Melbourne Wellington
Cape Town Nairobi Dar es Salaam Lusaka
Addis Abada Kuala Lumpur Singapore Hong Kong Tokyo

ISBN 0 19 831132 X

Printed in Great Britain by Thomson Litho Ltd., East Kilbride, Scotland.

A note about the book

Its purpose is to help O-level English Language students to improve their technique.

The emphasis is on the force of examples. As everyone knows, an example will often clarify, in a moment, what no amount of theory will ever make clear. So throughout the book I have used passages of literature to help me explain to the students what they need to understand.

What is a sentence? That, it seems to me, is the most important matter of all. If a student learns to understand *that*, a good many other things will come right too. And if he doesn't, nothing much will. So that is where we begin.

An opinion about the teaching of English

If a person's technical skill is poor he will not be able to write clearly, or logically, or interestingly. It may be that he is gifted with a vivid imagination: well, he will not be able to do it justice. So the important thing is to help him to improve his technique.

But there is more to it than that. Helping a person to improve the technique of his writing is the one sure way of helping him to improve its content. For a thought only becomes perfectly clear when it is expressed in perfectly clear language. And an imaginative idea—though it may have been conceived in a flash of insight—only takes shape as the writer searches for the most vivid way of expressing it.

So to try to teach someone how to write English by concentrating on the content of his work, without bothering very much about the craft, is to let him down badly. It deprives him of his education.

Contents

Choosing words
Daphne du Maurier: *The Birds*

Ways of going wrong
Graham Greene: *The Power and the Glory*

Sentences, full stops, and commas

Extracts taken from

Antonia Fraser:
Mary, Queen of Scots

1 Sentences and main verbs

What is a sentence? Here is one. It comes from Antonia Fraser's book, *Mary, Queen of Scots:*

Mary placed her hand on the New Testament.

That is a sentence because it is a complete statement. At the heart of it lies the verb—*placed*. *Placed*, as it is used there, is said to be a main verb because it brings a sentence into being. Here are some more sentences:

She solemnly declared herself to be innocent.

What word is the main verb in that one?

They offered her the services of the Dean of Peterborough, to help her make ready for her end.

And in that one?

The queen asked at what hour the execution would be. Shrewsbury replied in a faltering voice, 'At eight o'clock tomorrow morning.' Mary's servants, in a state of hysteria, begged for some sort of reprieve or at least a stay of execution, weeping and crying and protesting that the time was too short. Bourgoing, the queen's physician, pleaded with Shrewsbury, recalling how he had cured him of his illness. Shrewsbury said there was to be no delay.

There are five sentences in that passage. Will you now write down the main verb of each one.

1   *The servants weeping.* That is not a sentence because *weeping* is not a main verb. *The servants wept. Wept* is a main verb, and that is a sentence. Now here are three more groups of words which are not sentences because the verbs in them are not main verbs. Will you turn each group into a sentence by changing the verb into a main verb—just as we did in that example:

The servants protesting that the time was too short.

Bourgoing recalling the many occasions on which he had helped Shrewsbury.

Mary's old porter falling on his knees and beginning to pray.

2   *The servants in a state of hysteria.* That is not a sentence: there is no verb at all. *The servants were in a state of hysteria. Were* is a verb, and in this case it is a main verb, and it turns those words into a sentence. Now turn these groups of words into sentences by making the same change as the one we made there:

The servants terribly upset.

The old porter beside himself with grief.

Bourgoing quite unable to restrain his tears.

3   Look at the first and second sentences of the extract. Then try to imagine the queen's reaction to Shrewsbury's reply. (A slight change of expression? Some gesture or move-ment?) Describe her reaction in one sentence. Write the sentence in such a way that it could be fitted into Antonia Fraser's book immediately after Shrewsbury's words.

4   Look again at the third sentence of the passage, and then in a few sentences of your own, which would fit in after that one, describe in detail what you imagine two of the servants did after at that moment. (Did one kneel down? Did the other wring her hands? . . .) Call them Jane Kennedy and Elizabeth Curle, who were the best loved of the queen's servants. When you have finished, go through what you have written to make sure that all your sentences are complete and that each one ends with a full stop.

5   Now read the passage from Antonia Fraser's book again, including in it the sentences you have written for Questions 3 and 4; and as you read, notice how each sentence has the feeling of being a complete statement.

2 Verbs that consist of more than one word

Verbs have different tenses. *Jane Kennedy loves the queen*—the present. *Jane Kennedy loved the queen*—the past. *She prayed for her*—the past again.

Those two tenses—the simple present and the simple past—are the only two we can form in that neat way, by using just one word that we change slightly. To form any of the others we have to make use of small words like *is, was, will, have, do, did, would, may,* and *might*. These words are called auxiliary verbs, and whenever we use them we get a verb that consists of more than one word:

Jane Kennedy is praying for the queen. She will pray for her. She has been praying for her. She may have been praying for her. The queen was loved by her servants.

Will you write those sentences out and underline the verbs. They may consist of two words, or three, or four.

Quite often other words come in between the words that make up the verb:

The queen was dearly loved by her servants. She had always been dearly loved by them. Shrewsbury did not treat her very courteously. Jane Kennedy had often prayed for the queen's safety.

Now write out those sentences and underline the verbs.

The queen of Scots was left alone to spend the last evening of her life with her servants. Some of them like Jane Kennedy had spent a whole generation in her service. The queen bestowed numerous little personal objects on all her servants. Bourgoing received rings, silver boxes, and her music book bound in velvet to remind him of the many musical evenings of the captivity. Elizabeth Curle received miniatures set in gold, and enamelled tablets of Mary, Francis II, and James. Melville received a little tablet of gold, set with another portrait of James.

The queen lay on her bed without undressing. She did not try to sleep. Her women gathered round her, already wearing their black garments of mourning. Throughout the night the sound of hammering came from the great hall.

---

1   There are ten sentences in that passage, and each of them has one main verb in it. Write down the ten main verbs. Three of them consist of two words, and in one instance the two words are separated by another word.

2   When the queen asked Shrewsbury when the execution would be, he replied: *At eight o'clock tomorrow morning*. By adding *It . . .* at the beginning, and by putting in a main verb that consists of two words, turn his reply into a complete sentence.

3   Who was doing what, to cause the sound of the hammering? Answer in one sentence only, and underline its main verb, which will probably consist of two words.

4   *Her women wearing their black garments of mourning.* That is not a sentence because the word *wearing*, by itself, is not a main verb. *Her women were wearing their black garments of mourning. Were wearing* is a main verb; so that is a sentence. Will you now rewrite this next passage in such a way that it consists entirely of complete sentences. The alterations you will need to make will all be similar to the one we made just now:

It was a sad scene that the sheriff came upon when he entered. Mary standing silently at one end of the room. At the other end her servants whispering together, their faces pale and drawn. In the corner, scarcely visible in the dim light, the queen's physician praying quietly.

5   In a passage which could follow straight on from the last sentence of the extract on the opposite page, describe some other sound—or sounds—that might have been heard in the queen's room during the night, and also any slight incidents that might have occurred. (Perhaps one of the servants dozed off? Perhaps the moon rose and shone into the room? . . .) Let it be a passage of up to half a page long, and when you have finished it read it through to make sure that every sentence is a complete statement.

3   Main clauses

So the short night passed. At six o'clock, long before light, the queen rose. She distributed her purses, and gave her women a farewell embrace. Then she went into her little oratory* and prayed alone. She looked extremely pale, but she remained quite composed. Bourgoing handed her a little bread and wine to sustain her. The day now dawned fine and sunny. Between eight and nine a loud knocking sounded at the door, and a messenger shouted through it.

She distributed her purses, and gave her women a farewell embrace.

In that sentence Antonia Fraser has used an *and* to introduce a second main verb: *distributed . . . and . . . gave.*
The group of words that clusters round a main verb is called a main clause. *She distributed her purses*—that is a main clause. . . . *(she) gave her women a farewell embrace*—that is another one. So that sentence, as a whole, consists of two main clauses joined by an *and*.

She looked extremely pale, but she remained quite composed.

In that sentence the author has used a *but* to introduce a second main verb: *looked . . . but . . . remained.*
Each of those two main verbs has its group of words clustering round it; so here again we have a sentence consisting of two main clauses. But this time they are joined by a *but*.

    And and *but* are conjunctions, and they are often used in this way, to link main clauses together.

*a prayer room

1   What other sentence in that passage, besides the two we have just been looking at, have more than one main clause? Say which they are by writing down their main verbs; and between the verbs write down the conjunction that links them.

2   *Bourgoing handed her a little bread and wine to sustain her.* Write a sentence, which could be fitted into Antonia Fraser's book at this point, describing what the queen did in response. Write it in such a way that it contains two main clauses linked by an *and*. Underline the two main verbs and the *and*.

3   Now imagine that she made a different response, and let it be one that can be described in a sentence consisting of two main clauses linked by a *but*. Describe it in a sentence of this kind, and then underline the two main verbs and the *but*.

4   *The queen lay down on her bed, her women gathered round her, and the time of waiting began.*

That sentence consists of three main clauses linked by two *and*s; but only the last *and* is written in—a comma is put in place of the earlier one. That is what is usually done in a sentence of this kind. Now make up a similar sentence, with three main clauses in it, describing three events that might have occurred one after the other during that night in the queen's room.

5   What word is the main verb in the first sentence of the extract? And in the second one? And in the one beginning *Bourgoing . . . ?* and in the one after that?

6   *The day now dawned fine and sunny.* It was in February, and the queen was imprisoned in Fotheringay Castle—a grim fortress on the River Nene, in the flat Northamptonshire countryside. Imagine that there was a small slit of a window in her oratory, and that she glanced out of it for a moment that morning. In one paragraph describe what she saw. But before you do, read Antonia Fraser's paragraph again and notice how clear and simple her sentences are. Try to make yours equally clear.

4 Subordinate clauses

A group of words which is introduced by a word like *when* or *because* or *although* or *that*, is called a subordinate clause.

When the sheriff entered . . .

A subordinate clause can never from a sentence on its own because it is not a complete statement. It must always attach itself to a main clause.

When the sheriff entered he found Mary kneeling quietly in prayer.

In that sentence the main clause is *he found Mary kneeling quietly in prayer*. The main verb is *found*. *Entered* is not a main verb because it is introduced by a *when*, and that *when* downgrades it into being just the verb of a subordinate clause.

Words like *when* are called subordinating conjunctions, because they link subordinate clauses to main clauses.

When the sheriff entered he found Mary kneeling quietly in prayer in front of the crucifix which hung above her altar. Her groom, Hannibal Stuart, now bore this crucifix before her, as she was escorted towards the great hall. When she reached the entry chamber to the hall her servants were held back from following her, and the queen was told she was to die quite alone, by the orders of Elizabeth.

Mary turned to Paulet and the lords and pleaded with them to allow at least her own servants to be with her at the death. Kent replied that before her execution her servants would be sure to cry out and upset the queen herself, as well as disquieting the company. 'My Lord,' replied Mary, 'I will promise they shall not do any such thing. Alas poor souls, it would do them good to bid me farewell.' After a consultation, the lords decided that Mary might have after all the choice of six of her servants to accompany her.

---

1   Here is a sentence that consists of a subordinate clause followed by a main clause:

Although Shrewsbury was an obstinate man he gave way in the end.

Will you turn it into one that consists of two main clauses, by getting rid of the subordinating conjunction and introducing a *but*.

2   *The queen had her faith to sustain her and she remained serenely calm.*

That sentence consists of two main clauses. Turn it into one that consists of a main clause and a subordinate clause, by getting rid of the *and* and introducing a *because*. If you want to you can reverse the order in which the two ideas are expressed.

3   One subordinating conjunction—*that*—is sometimes left out: *Shrewsbury said that he was sorry for the delay. Shrewsbury said he was sorry for the delay.* Is there a *that* in the extract that could be left out? If you think there is, give the number of the line it comes in.

4   And is there a place in the extract where a *that* has been left out and where one could be put in? Again, if you think there is, give the line number.

5   What is the main verb in the second sentence of the extract? And in the last one?

6   Read the first sentence of the extract again, and then in a few sentences of your own describe the scene in detail, from your imagination. (What sort of crucifix was it? What was the altar like? And the room? . . .)

7   The lords told Mary that in refusing to allow her servants into the hall they were acting on Queen Elizabeth's orders. Antonia Fraser tells us this in the first paragraph. We feel fairly certain, after reading the second one, that they were lying. Why? Let your answer consist of a complete sentence. (If you begin it with *because* it will only consist of a subordinate clause.)

5   Relative clauses

. . . the lords decided that Mary might have after all the choice of six of her servants to accompany her. Thus Melville, Bourgoing, Gervais, and the old man Didier, who had been for many years Mary's porter, were allowed to go forward, together with the two dearest of Mary's women, Jane Kennedy and Elizabeth Curle, who shared her bed. Mary then went to follow the sheriff, having first bestowed a small gift (probably a seal) on Sir William Fitzwilliam, the castellan of Fotheringay, who had shown especial courtesy to her in the carrying-out of his office.

In that paragraph there are three clauses that begin with *who*. They called relative clauses. They are called that because the *who* relates back to a noun that has just been mentioned. The first *who* relates back to the old man Didier. Who does the second one relate back to? And the third one?

Who is one of a family of four words. The other three are *whom*, *whose*, and *which*. And sometimes, too, the word *that* joins this family—when it is used instead of *which*. They all introduce relative clauses, by relating back to a noun.

This last letter from the King of France, which arrived on the 7th of February, was never given to the queen.

What noun does the *which* relate back to in that sentence?

She knelt down in front of the wooden crucifix that hung above the altar.

What noun does the *that* relate back to? Could we write *which* instead of it?

Relative clauses can never form a sentence on their own. They are subordinate clauses, and must always attach themselves to a main clause.

Which deeply distressed the queen.

That is not a sentence.

This ill-mannered reply, which deeply distressed the queen, was typical of Paulet's behaviour towards her.

That is.

1   Here is a sentence that consists of two main clauses. Will you change it into one that consists of a relative clause and a main clause. Do not change the word order. You will need to leave out two words and add a *who*.

Didier was now a very old man, and he scarcely seemed to know what was happening.

2   Here are three more sentences, each consisting of two main clauses. Again, will you change each one into a sentence that consists of a relative clause and a main clause. Do not alter the word order. You will need a *who*, a *whose*, and a *which* (but not in that order).

The queen's trial had been conducted in great haste and it was a travesty of justice.

Shrewsbury was an obstinate man, and he refused to listen to this very reasonable argument.

Sir William's kindness had brought Mary much comfort, and he received a special gift.

3   Sometimes *whom*, *which*, and *that* can be left out. Your ear will tell you when they can be. They can be left out in three of the next five sentences. Will you write out these three sentences again, leaving out the word in each case. In one of the sentences you will need to make a slight change in the order of the words.

The letter that arrived on the 2nd of February was from the King of France.

The man whom Mary despised most was the earl of Kent.

The room in which Mary now found herself was narrow and cramped.

The only thing about it that pleased her was the view.

The letter which Melville wrote was never delivered.

4   Explain what is wrong with this next sentence, and then write it out again with the mistake put right. None of the words needs to be altered—only the order of them:

Mary confided a secret to Sir William as soon as she heard that the Court had published the names of the conspirators, which he promised never to reveal.

5   Make up a sentence with the word *whom* in it. And then one with *whose* in it.

6 Participle phrases (-*ing*)

The queen now entered the great hall in silence. The
spectators, gazing with awe at this legendary figure, saw a
tall and gracious woman who at first sight seemed to be
dressed entirely in black, save for the long white veil and the
white head-dress. She held a crucifix and a prayer-book in
her hand, and two rosaries hung down from her waist.
Round her neck was a pomander chain and an Agnus Dei.
Despite the fact that Mary's shoulders were now bowed with
illness, she walked with immense dignity. Time and suffering
had long ago rubbed away the delicate youthful charm of her
face, but to many of the spectators her extraordinary
composure and serenity had its own beauty.

If you look again at the second sentence of that paragraph
you will see that it contains a group of words that are set
apart from the rest of it:

. . . *gazing with awe at this legendary figure* . . .

Groups of words like those, introduced by a word that ends
in -*ing*, are called participle phrases. Here is another one
(forming the first part of the sentence):

*Holding her crucifix in her hand, the queen walked up the
steps.*

A participle phrase is always associated with a noun.
That one is associated with the queen. It tells us something
about her which we are to bear in mind when we come to the
main point of the sentence—which is that she walked up the
steps.

And now will you look back to the first participle phrase
we mentioned—beginning *gazing with awe*—and say what
noun it is associated with.

1   *Then the queen closed her eyes and tried to sleep.*

That sentence consists of two main clauses. We will turn it into one that consists of a participle phrase and a main clause:

Then, closing her eyes, the queen tried to sleep.

Will you now rewrite each of the following sentences in such a way as to bring about the same change:

The lords thought that the queen might try to kill herself, and they ordered the sheriff to break the door open.

A shaft of moonlight moved like a clock's hand across the wall and marked the slow passing of the night.

Mary placed her hand on the New Testament and protested her innocence.

2   A participle phrase must always go with the *right* noun. Here is one that doesn't:

Hannibal Stuart walked in front of the queen, glancing neither to the right nor left and holding her head proudly.

Will you correct that piece of writing. Re-shape it in any way you like. For example, you may decide that it is better not to use a participle phrase at all.

3   And here is another piece of writing to correct:

Walking slowly down the aisle between the rows of benches, the spectators sitting in the front had a clear view of the expression on the queen's face.

4   The last sentence of the extract consists of two main clauses. Write down the two main verbs, and also—putting it between them—the conjunction that links them.

5   In a few sentences describe in detail, from your imagination, Mary's ageing face. When you have finished, read through what you have written, to make sure that all your sentences are complete.

7 Participle phrases (-*ed*)

*Then, watched by the huge crowd of silent spectators, the
queen mounted the scaffold.*

Watched by the huge crowd of silent spectators is another
kind of participle phrase. This kind, too, is always associated
with a noun. The one we have just looked at is associated
with the queen. It tells us something about her which we are
to bear in mind when we read that she mounted the scaffold.

There is one point to notice. With the first kind of
participle phrase the introductory word always ends in -*ing*.
But the word that introduces the second kind does not always
end in -*ed*. This is because some verbs are irregular. *Watch*
turns into *watched*, but *leave* turns into *left*, *wear* into *worn*,
speak into *spoken*, and so on. So if we make up participle
phrases that are introduced by words like those, this is what
we get:

*The queen, left alone with her servants, whispered a few words
of comfort to them.*

*The old porter, worn down with age and anxiety, followed
wearily behind.*

*These words, spoken in anger, had a very damaging effect on
the queen's cause.*

In the centre of the great hall, which lay on the ground
floor of the castle, directly below the room in which Mary
had been tried, was set a wooden stage, hung with black. It
was about twelve feet square, and two feet high off the
ground. Within the precincts of the stage were two stools for
Shrewsbury and Kent. Beside them was placed, about two
feet high, also draped in black, the block, and a little
cushioned stool on which it was intended that the queen
should sit while she was disrobed. The great axe was already
lying there—'like those with which they cut wood' said
Bourgoing later. A huge blaze had been lit in the fireplace
against the cold of the great hall.

---

1 Participle phrases of the *-ed* kind must go with the right noun—just as those of the *-ing* kind must. Here is one that doesn't:

Kept closely guarded in one narrow wing of the castle, many people thought it a scandal that the queen of Scotland should be treated in such a way.

Will you correct that piece of writing. Re-shape it in any way you like. You needn't use a participle phrase at all if you think it better not to.

2 And here is another piece of writing to correct. Again, you will need to re-shape it:

Situated at the far end of the hall and partly concealed behind the rows of spectators, Elizabeth Curle found it difficult to see how high the scaffold was.

3 Will you change the next sentence, which consists of two main clauses, into one that consists of a main clause and a relative clause:

The block was draped in black and was about two feet high.

4 And now change these three sentences in the same way:

The earl of Kent had a very short temper, and he replied curtly that he could not grant her request.

Fotheringay Castle had been built in the 11th century, and it was one of the grimmest fortresses in the whole of England.

Old man Didier had been Mary's porter for many years, and to him the news came like a death-blow.

5 What is the main verb of the last sentence of the extract? (It consists of three words.)

6 In a paragraph of between five and ten lines describe a room—any room you like, imaginary or real. Try to describe it in much it in much the same way as Antonia Fraser describes the hall at Fotheringay—that is, in a style that is dignified and factual.

15

8   Incomplete sentences

Sometimes a writer, in order to achieve an effect of briskness, will write incomplete sentences. Antonia Fraser might perhaps have written something like this:

Nearly ten o'clock on the morning of the 8th of February, 1587. The great hall crowded with spectators. In the centre, a wooden stage, draped with black. At the far end a huge fire burning brightly.

Those sentences are all incomplete because in each case the main verb has been left out. The incompleteness makes it seem that the scene is being sketched in a few rapid strokes, and this adds a touch of drama.

But there is another kind of incompleteness:

In Tudor times criminals had to suffer cruel punishments. The stocks, for example. Or public floggings. Showing how uncivilised life was in those days.

That kind of incompleteness is quite a different matter. The person who wrote that was not after some special effect: he expressed himself in that disjointed way because he allowed the easy-going habits of everyday speech to take over his writing. When we speak we use language more casually: we abbreviate, we stop for long pauses, and we miss words out. As a result many of our sentences are left incomplete. It is not a good idea to write in that way.

The executioners, helped by Jane Kennedy and Elizabeth Curle, assisted the queen to undress. Stripped of her black, she stood in her red petticoat, and it was seen that above it she wore a red satin bodice. It was notable that she neither wept nor changed her calm and almost happy expression. She even remarked wryly of the executioners that she had never before had such grooms of the chamber to make her ready. It was the queen's women who could not contain their lamentations as they wept and crossed themselves and muttered snatches of Latin prayers. Finally Mary had to turn to them and, remembering her promise to Shrewsbury that they would not weep aloud if they were admitted to the hall, she admonished them softly in French: 'Ne crie point pour moi. J'ai promis pour vous.'

1   Will you look back to that first piece of writing on the opposite page (beginning *Nearly ten o'clock . . .*) and rewrite it in the form of complete sentences. Keep it exactly the same except for putting a main verb in each sentence.

2   Now here is the whole of that other, disjointed piece of writing. Rewrite it in the form of complete sentences, and in fluent English. Re-shape it as much as you like, but don't alter the meaning:

In Tudor times criminals had to suffer cruel punishments. The stocks, for example. Or public floggings. Showing how uncivilised life was in those days. The situation is quite different today. No corporal punishment now. And hanging has been abolished. There are also open prisons. A great advance this. With the prisoners not locked up but put on trust. Because it has been realised that not all criminals are the same. Some needing to be educated rather than punished.

3   In that piece of writing why is the last sentence an incomplete one? If you can't answer turn back to page 10.

4   *The queen took Jane by the hand and led the way into the oratory.*

Will you turn that sentence, which consists of two main clauses, into one that consists of a participle phrase followed by a main clause.

5   What does *wryly* mean, as it is used in the fourth sentence of the extract?

6   What is the force of *even*, in the same sentence?

7   Can you translate the French—even if you don't know any?

9   Full stops

The time had come for Jane Kennedy to bind the queen's eyes with the white cloth. She kissed the cloth and then wrapped it gently round her mistress's eyes. The two women then withdrew from the stage. The queen knelt down on the cushion in front of the block. Then, feeling for the block, she laid her head down upon it, placing her chin carefully with both her hands, so that if one of the executioners had not moved them back they too would have lain in the direct line of the axe. When the queen was lying there quite motionless, Bull's assistant put his hand on the body to steady it for the blow. Even so, the first blow, as it fell, missed the neck and cut into the back of the head. The queen's lips moved, and her servants thought they heard the whispered words, 'Sweet Jesus'. The second blow severed the neck. It was about ten o'clock in the morning of Wednesday the 8th of February. The queen of Scots was then aged forty-four, and in the nineteenth year of her English captivity.

In that paragraph the commas show where the sentences pause, the full stops where they end. That is what commas and full stops always do. They work in partnership—one indicating the pauses, the other indicating the endings.

The worst punctuation mistake is to cut across that simple division of labour and use a comma to mark the end of a sentence. Anyone who does that as regular practice will be likely to write very muddled English.

Jane Kennedy gently wrapped the cloth round the queen's eyes, the two women then withdrew from the stage.

The comma there doesn't cause any confusion because both the sentences happen to be simple ones. It just looks bad. But a comma at the end of a sentence very often *will* cause confusion:

Then the queen entered the hall, with a gasp of surprise, for they had expected her to be entirely in black, the spectators saw that she was wearing a white veil.

1   Will you write out the wrongly punctuated passage we have just looked at and put it right.

2   Here is a passage in which the ends of all the sentences have been marked by commas instead of full stops. Rewrite it and punctuate it correctly. Then turn back to page 6 to see if you have punctuated in the same way as Antonia Fraser has:

So the short night passed, at six o'clock, long before light, the queen rose, she distributed her purses, and gave her women a farewell embrace, then she went into her little oratory and prayed alone, she looked extremely pale, but she remained quite composed, Bourgoing handed her a little bread and wine to sustain her, the day now dawned fine and sunny, between eight and nine a loud knocking sounded at the door, and a messenger shouted through it.

3   Here is a sentence that consists of two main clauses:

Then she felt for the block and laid her head down upon it.

Will you change it into one that consists of a participle phrase and a main clause. When you have done that, look again at the extract on the opposite page and compare what you have written with what Antonia Fraser put.

4   Here is another sentence that consists of two main clauses:

The spectators saw a tall and gracious woman, and at first sight she seemed to be dressed entirely in black.

Will you change it into one that consists of a main clause followed by a relative clause. Then look back to the second sentence of the extract on page 12.

5   There is a subordinate clause in the fifth sentence of the extract on the opposite page. The subordinating conjunction which introduces it is *so that*. What is its verb? It consists of three words. (But look at the next question before you answer this one.)

6   This clause contains, within itself, another subordinate clause. Quote this inner subordinate clause.

7   The last two sentences of the extract make a contrast to the rest of it, and they give the paragraph a firm, dignified ending. Explain what sort of contrast it is.

10   Putting an *and* instead of a full stop

We must be careful never to join together, by using an *and*, what should be two separate sentences.

With the first light of the morning the queen went into her oratory in order to pray alone and it was one of those days in early February when it suddenly seems possible that the spring will come.

The *and* there isn't right. Our ear tells us it isn't. It makes it sound as though the writer tried to get out everything he had to say in one breath.

When the queen asked at what hour she was to die, Shrewsbury replied that it was to be tomorrow morning at eight o'clock and the queen begged him to allow her body to be buried in France.

That one isn't right either. The writer seems to end up in a place where he never expected to be.

Will you now write out those two passages as they ought to have been written. Only a very small alteration is needed, in each case, to put them right.

In the great hall of Fotheringay, before the wondering eyes of the crowd, the executioner now held aloft the dead woman's head, crying out as he did so: 'God save the queen.' The lips still moved and continued to do so for a quarter of an hour after the death. But at this moment the auburn tresses in his hand came apart from the skull and the head itself fell to the ground. It was seen that Mary Stuart's own hair had in fact been quite grey, and very short at the time of her death; for her execution she had chosen to wear a wig. The spectators were stunned by the unexpected sight. It was left to the dean of Peterborough to call out strongly: 'So perish all the Queen's enemies', and for Kent, standing over the corpse, to echo: 'Such be the end of all the Queen's and all the Gospel's enemies.' But Shrewsbury could not speak, and his face was wet with tears.

---

1   Here are four sentences. In two of them *and* is used badly. Will you write those out again and correct what is wrong—by leaving out the *and* and putting a full stop instead:

Bourgoing offered the queen a little wine, and she accepted it gladly.

The queen spent her last evening with her servants, and some of them had been in her service for nearly a generation.

Finally, before she retired to rest, the queen wrote a letter to her brother-in-law and it was dated the 8th of February, 1587.

Throughout the night the sound of hammering came from the great hall, and the tramp of the guards' boots could be heard outside the door.

2   Here are four passages. Each one consists of a pair of sentences. Some would still read perfectly well if the full stop at the end of the first sentence were changed to a comma and an *and* were put in after it. Others wouldn't. Rewrite those that would, putting in the comma and the *and*.

After a few moments there was a loud knocking at the door. This was followed by the sound of tramping feet in the passage outside.

The queen arose as soon as it was light. It was a fine clear morning.

In her hand she held a prayer-book. Two rosaries hung down from her waist.

A gang of workmen had been working hard all night to erect the wooden stage. It was about twelve feet square and two feet high.

3   The last sentence of the extract consists of two main clauses. Will you re-arrange it so that it consists of a relative clause (introduced by *whose*) and a main clause. You will have to reverse the order in which the two ideas are expressed.

4   *The spectators were stunned by the unexpected sight* (line 10). Picture the reactions of a few individual spectators, and describe them in a paragraph of between five and ten lines. Try to write your description in such a way that it would not seem out of place in Antonia Fraser's book.

11 Commas

A comma—just one, on its own—marks a pause. But commas can also be used in pairs. A pair of commas encloses a group of words and sets them aside from the rest of the sentence. It may be a subordinate clause they enclose:

Between eight and nine, soon after the queen had finished her prayers, a loud knocking was heard at the door.

Or a participle phrase:

The Earl of Shrewsbury, thinking that Mary's servants would be unable to restrain their tears, refused to allow them into the hall.

Or it may be a group of words of some other kind. Sometimes it is just a single word:

But this, unfortunately, was not to be.

There is one mistake that is always being made. In some cases we don't pause at all for the first of the two enclosing commas, and so it gets missed out. It mustn't be.

The queen, however, was badly treated.   Her room, for example, was narrow and cramped.   Her servants, it seems, knew nothing about the existence of this letter.   This, then, was the conclusion she came to.

In each of those sentences the first comma is working in partnership with the second one to form an enclosing pair, even though we don't pause for it.

It was now time for the executioner to strip the body of its remaining adornments before handing it over to the embalmers. But at this point the queen's little lap dog, which had managed to accompany her into the hall under her long skirts, crept out from beneath her petticoat and, in its distress, stationed itself piteously beneath the severed head and shoulders of the body. Nor would it be coaxed away, but steadfastly and uncomprehendingly clung to the solitary thing it could find in the hall which still reminded it of its mistress.

---

1 Make up a sentence that contains a participle phrase enclosed by a pair of commas.

2 . . . And now one containing a subordinate clause enclosed by commas.

3 . . . And now one containing a relative clause enclosed by commas.

4 Can you make up a sentence which contains a single word enclosed by a pair of commas? The word mustn't be *unfortunately* or *however* or *then*, because we used those three on the opposite page.

5 The second sentence of the extract has two main clauses in it. Write down the main verb of each one, and also— putting it between them—the conjunction that links them.

6 This sentence contains one other clause too. What kind of clause is it?

7 In a few sentences, which could be added to the end of the extract, describe the dog's behaviour while it was stationed beside its dead mistress; and then describe how Bull, the executioner, dragged it away.

8 Here is a passage which is very disjoined because many of the sentences are incomplete. Rewrite it in the form of complete sentences, so that it reads fluently. Re-arrange it as much as you like, but without altering the meaning:

The queen was not well treated at Fotheringay. Only a few servants. And not all those her own choice. And her rooms were small and sparsely furnished. She was allowed very little freedom. Not even permitted to take the air unless she was accompanied by a guard. A completely unnecessary precaution this, since it would have been against her own interests to try to escape. But the lords insisted on it. Anything to make life unpleasant for her. The reason being that they hated her religion.

12   Commas and relative clauses

Relative clauses must sometimes be enclosed between commas, and at other times they must not be. It depends on the sense.

The queen's personal maid, who had served her for many years, was not allowed to accompany her to Fotheringay.

There, the relative clause is set aside from the main flow of the sentence. That is because what it tells us is not an essential point, but just a piece of information put in as an extra. Relative clauses of this kind, which just add a comment, are called commenting clauses, and they must always be enclosed by commas.

But no commas at all must be put if the clause is *not* set aside.

The girl who looked after the queen at Fotheringay was a complete stranger.

That one isn't. It can't be, because it plays an essential part in the meaning. It makes clear—or defines—which girl the writer is talking about. Clauses like that are called defining clauses, and they are never enclosed between commas.

At Fotheringay now it was as if a murder had taken place. The weeping women in the hall were pushed away and locked in their rooms. The castle gates were locked, so that no one could leave and break the news to the outside world. The blood-stained block was burnt. Every object which might be associated with the queen of Scots was burnt, scoured or washed, so that not a trace of her blood might remain to create a holy relic. At four o'clock in the afternoon the body was further stripped, and the organs, including the heart, were removed and handed to the sheriff, who had them buried secretly deep within the castle of Fotheringay. The exact spot was never revealed. The body was then wrapped in a wax winding-sheet and incarcerated in a heavy lead coffin.

Only Shrewsbury's eldest son, Lord Talbot, was allowed to gallop forth from the castle at about one o'clock, hard toward London, to break the news of what had taken place that morning to Elizabeth.

---

1   These are some of the objects that were destroyed after the execution, for fear of their becoming holy relics: the crucifix carried by Hannibal Stuart, the queen's shoes, her wig, her veil, her prayer-book, her pomander chain, her golden rosary. Pick out three of them and make up a sentence about each one. Let each sentence contain a relative clause enclosed between commas.

The word *sheriff*, in the first paragraph of the extract, is followed by a comma and then by the word *who*. Can you make up a sentence which also contains these two words, coming one immediately after the other, but with no comma between them? You will only be able to do it by using the relative clause to show which sheriff you mean.

3   *Shrewsbury was afraid that the queen's servants would break down and weep, and so he did not want to allow them to enter the hall.*

Will you change that sentence (which consists of two main clauses) into one that consists of a main clause followed by a subordinate clause. You will have to reverse the order in which the two ideas are expressed and also re-arrange the wording very slightly.

4   Imagine that there is an asterisk after the word *revealed* (towards the end of the first paragraph), and make up a footnote to go with it. Begin like this: *'In fact it was discovered, quite by chance, only a few years ago. A workman . . .'* Let your footnote be between five and ten lines long.

5   Read again the first five lines of the extract and notice how firm and clear the writing is. In sentences that are equally strong describe the unlocking of the castle gates and the departure of Lord Talbot. When you have finished, go through what you have written and underline the main verbs.

13   Putting too much into one sentence

People never make their sentences too short. It is not
possible to. *He refused.*—that is a perfectly good sentence.
But they often make them too long.

Usually, when they do, it is because they have tried to say
several things at once in one sentence, instead of saying them
separately in two or three. So the thing that is wrong with
the long sentence they write is not the length of it but the
muddle it's in.

Never overcrowd a sentence by cramming too many
thoughts or facts into it. As soon as you come to a natural
stopping-place put a full stop.

Lord Talbot reached the capital next morning at nine. The
queen was at Greenwich. When she was told the news she
received it at first with great indignation, and then with
terrible distress. She turned like an angry snake on the
secretary Davison and had him thrown into prison for
daring to use the execution warrant. She maintained that she
had only signed it 'for safety's sake' and had merely given it
to Davison to keep, not to use. Unlike its queen, London
itself suffered from no such doubts. The bells were rung,
and fires were lighted in the streets.

Notice how clear those sentences are. In all except two of
them just one central thought is expressed, and then the full
stop comes. In those two the first thought leads on to the
next one so naturally that the author continues with an *and*.

1   Here is a piece of writing in which the writer has crowded too much into one sentence. Re-write it, making three sentences of it. You will have to alter the wording very slightly.

Fotheringay Castle, which is now only a mound of grass, stood on the banks of the River Nene in the flat Northamptonshire countryside, and the sight of it, from whatever direction you approached it, would have had a depressing effect on the spirits, its most conspicuous feature being its lofty keep, which was so gaunt and forbidding that it must have seemed a perfect place for torturing and murdering people.

2   And here is another passage that needs to be improved in the same way. Again, divide it into three sentences:

To Mary the most important room in her set of apartments was her oratory, which was a small cell-like cubicle, lit only by a slit of a window which faced towards the river, and in this room on the evening of her arrival she placed her altar and crucifix.

3   And here is another. Divide this one into two sentences:

On hearing the news of the execution Elizabeth flew into a rage and immediately had Davison thrown into prison which was an irresponsible act, because he had only been carrying out orders which she herself had given.

4   Write out, in full, the subordinate clause that forms part of the third sentence of the extract.

5   There are two main verbs in the last sentence, joined by an *and*. Which are they?

6   Lord Talbot, who was a young man, was ushered into Queen Elizabeth's presence in Greenwich Palace . . . he delivered his message . . . the queen received the news at first with grief and then with anger. Picture the scene, and describe it in detail.

14   Varying the length of your sentences

Nothing is more dreary to read than a passage of writing that consists of long sentence after long sentence, with no relief. It tires the reader. Try, now and then, to vary the length of your sentences. The variety will give a touch of life to your writing. This is not to say that from now on you should look at every sentence you write in order to make sure that it's not the same length as the one before: but simply that you should occasionally give a thought to the matter, and not write a whole series of long sentences without any idea that your English is getting heavier and heavier to read.

The most effective contrast is the one that comes when a very short sentence is introduced. In this next passage, for example, the fourth sentence comes in very well. It lifts the writing up, as it were, and lightens the whole feeling of it.

But at Fotheringay itself nothing was changed. It was as though the castle, cut off from the rest of the world, had fallen asleep. The queen's farewell letters to the Pope remained unposted and undelivered, lingering in the hands of her household. Spring turned to summer. The snowdrops which had scattered the meadows round the River Nene on the day of her death gave place to purple thistles, sometimes romantically called Queen Mary's tears. Still the body of the dead queen, embalmed and wrapped in its heavy lead coffin, was given no burial.

---

1   Rewrite this sentence in such a way as to divide it into two sentences, with the first one long and the second one short—and notice how the contrast strengthens the writing:

The sheriff, who had been warned that Mary was in a highly nervous state and might become hysterical, was surprised at what he saw when he entered her room, because she was kneeling quietly in prayer.

2   Now divide this passage into three sentences, with the middle one very short:

When Elizabeth received the news of Mary's execution she was deeply distressed and she turned aside and wept, and her servants were amazed, because never before had they seen her show her emotions in this way in the presence of other people.

3   Divide this passage into four sentences, making the third one very short:

It had been Mary's wish that she should be buried in France, and Elizabeth had received several letters from her during the period of the trial and was fully aware that she had made this request, but it was not granted because after a delay of nearly six months she was buried in Peterborough Cathedral.

Is it better to keep the *but* in, or leave it out?

4   And now divide this passage into four sentences, making both the first one and the last one very short:

It was a wet November day, with the mist hanging so thickly over the castle that it hid the great keep from sight, and a damp haze filling the queen's apartments, and streams of moisture running down the walls of her bedroom, so that her servants feared for her health.

Punctuation

Extracts taken from

D. H. Lawrence:
The White Stocking

15 Colons

A colon, like a full stop, marks the end of a sentence. But it does it in a special way: it tells us that in the next sentence the writer is going to explain what he has just said. So as well as making us pause, it urges us forward.

This novel has one serious weakness: it lacks humour.

We lower the voice right down for a full stop, to a full close. We don't for a colon: we keep it still raised, to show that although we have completed a sentence we have not completed the point we are making.

The rain increased our difficulties in two ways: it reduced the visibility and made the path very slippery.

We soon discovered how the thief had got in: a large hole had been cut in the lower part of the door.

Colons are also used to direct the attention forward in a more obvious way, after expressions like these: *The following points were made: Here is an example: This is how the letter ran:*   There, the colons just mean 'as follows'.

Sam Adams was a bachelor of forty, growing stout, a man well dressed and florid, with a large brown moustache and thin hair. His fondness for the girls, or the fondness of the girls for him, was notorious. Elsie—quick, pretty—had a great attraction for him. He would come into the warehouse dressed in a rather sporting jacket, of fawn colour, in trousers of fine black-and-white check, and with a scarlet carnation in his button-hole, to impress her. But she had a reservation about him: he was too loud for her good taste.

Meanwhile Whiston was courting her. He was a shapely young fellow of about twenty-eight. . . .

---

1   Why is there a colon, instead of a full stop, after the last sentence but one of the first paragraph?

2   In five of the following passages a colon is needed after the first of the two sentences, to show that in the second one the writer is going to explain what he has just said, or complete the point of it. So the full stop that has been put is either wrong, or not as good as a colon would be. Write those five passages out again, putting colons:

But Sam Adams had one quality which made many women dislike him. He was terribly conceited.

Elsie was a pretty girl. She was also extemely intelligent and quick-witted.

The reason why she was working late was quite obvious. She was hoping that Sam Adams would offer to take her home.

It was not surprising that he couldn't remember what had happened. He had been hopelessly drunk.

She soon guessed what was in his mind. He was thinking she'd invented the whole story.

He was always very well dressed. Some of the girls, however, thought that his taste was too loud.

But this at least could be said in his favour. He was never deliberately cruel.

3   Improve the punctuation of this passage by changing two of the full stops to colons. Write the passage out in full, with the improvements made:

Sam Adams had some irritating ways. Towards the end of every working day, for example, he always did the same impertinent thing. He went round asking each girl in turn if she'd like to come home with him. Elsie always went very red when it came to her turn to be asked. He had another irritating habit, too. He always laughed, loud and long, at his own jokes.

4   Make up two sentences about someone behaving rudely or thoughtlessly, and write them in such a way that the second one explains the first one, or completes the sense of it—so that you need to put a colon after the first one.

5   Now make up two more, also separated by a colon, about someone who is able to perform a feat of strength or a feat of intellectual skill.

16 Semicolons

A semicolon marks an ordinary pause at the end of a
sentence, without any of the forward urge that a colon
implies. In this respect it's like a full stop. But it's weaker
than a full stop, and ends a sentence less sharply. A writer
may perhaps use a semicolon when two sentences are closely
linked, and he wants only a slight break between them.

*She went back to that house once, many years later. It was a
sad sight. Nearly all the windows were broken; there was a
hole in the roof where the guttering had been torn away, and
in other places tiles were loose; the rain had been pouring in.*

You will hardly ever need semicolons. If you have only just
learnt how to use colons and find that enough to go on with,
it's quite a good idea to forget about semicolons, once you
have learnt what they are for.

At Christmas Sam Adams gave a party at his house, to
which he invited Elsie and Whiston.

Whiston called for her. Then she tripped along beside
him, holding her large cashmere shawl across her breast. He
strode with long strides, her silk shoes bulging the pockets of
his full-skirted overcoat.

They were rather late. Agitated with anticipation, in the
cloak-room she gave up her shawl, donned her silk shoes,
and looked at herself in the mirror. The loose bunches of
curls on either side of her face danced prettily; her mouth
smiled.

She hung a moment in the door of the brilliantly lighted
room. Many people were moving within the blaze of lamps,
under the crystal chandeliers, the full skirts of the women
balancing and floating, the side-whiskers and cravats of the
men bowing above. Then she entered the light.

In an instant Sam Adams was coming forward, lifting
both his arms in boisterous welcome.

'Come late, would you,' he shouted, 'like royalty?'

He seized her hands and led her forward. He opened his
mouth wide when he spoke, and the effect of the warm, dark
opening behind the brown whiskers was disturbing. But she
was floating into the throng on his arm.

---

1   Why did Lawrence put a semicolon, instead of a full stop, after the last sentence but one of the third paragraph?

2   In three of the following passages a colon is needed, and the semicolon that has been put there is wrong. Write those three out again, putting a colon:

The room was very crowded; at first the stuffy atmosphere and the noise made Elsie feel quite ill.

Sam Adams had one great advantage over Whiston; he was an excellent dancer.

He wrote down the following note on a scrap of paper; 'Play it next'.

All through the evening the same thought kept going through his mind; he didn't really care for her at all.

Whiston strode forward with long strides; Elsie tripped along beside him.

3   Now look at the end of the second paragraph. The obvious expression would have been *she smiled*. Lawrence wrote *her mouth smiled*. Do you think his expression is more vivid? If you do, explain in what way.

4   Write a short paragraph which could be fitted into Lawrence's book between the second and third paragraphs of the quoted passage. Let its purpose be to describe the course of the walk taken by Whiston and Elsie to Sam Adams's house (where they arrive at the beginning of the next paragraph). What did they pass? What sort of evening was it? . . . Try to include in your paragraph at least one semicolon.

5   Now write a passage, about five or six lines long, which would form a continuation of the fourth paragraph of the extract. Describe, in greater detail than Lawrence does, what Elsie saw when she *entered the light*.

17 Dashes, used singly

Dashes serve two purposes. A writer may use one to show that the vital piece of information, which will complete the sense of what he has just said, is about to come. The dash points forward to it:

Only one part of the mountain remained to be conquered—the north face.

By going to live in that remote place he found what he had been searching for—peace of mind.

Or he may use one to show that what follows it was added as an afterthought:

On our visits to these marshlands we found many rare specimens—rare, that is, for amateurs like us.

At last we were nearing the end of our journey—or so we thought.

'Now then,' said Sam Adams, taking Elsie's card to write down the dances, 'I've got *carte blanche*, haven't I?'

'Whiston doesn't dance,' she said.

'I am a lucky man!' he said, scribbling his initials. 'Now I'm set up, my darling, for the evening.'

Then, quick, always at his ease, he looked over the room. She waited in front of him. He was ready. Catching the eye of the band, he nodded. In a moment the music began.

'Now then, Elsie,' he said, and there was a curious caress in his voice that seemed to lap her body in a glow—a warm, delicious glow.

He was an excellent dancer. He seemed to draw her close in to him by some male warmth of attraction, so that she became all soft and pliant to him, flowing to his form. She was carried in a kind of strong, warm flood; her feet moved themselves, and only the music threw her away from him, threw her back to him, to his clasp, in his strong form moving against her, rhythmically, deliciously. When it was over, he was pleased and his eyes had a curious gleam which thrilled her.

---

1   What is the effect of the dash in the sentence that forms the fifth paragraph?

2   In five of the following sentences a dash is needed, rather than the comma that has been put. Write those five out again, putting a dash:

He looked at her strangely from time to time, with a curious gleam in his eye.

Whiston found Elsie's behaviour very irritating, so irritating, in fact, that he decided to leave.

But Sam Adams had another streak in his character which he carefully concealed, a streak of cruelty.

He was drunk, not completely, but enough to make him more aggressive than usual.

He decided that there was only one thing he could do to save his pride, leave immediately.

She waited a moment before stepping forward, because the band was not ready yet.

In this situation he resorted to his usual tactic, flattery.

Elsie still refused to answer, even though she could see that his temper was rising.

3   Punctuate this passage. As well as two more full stops and one more comma, you will need one colon and one dash:

The dance seemed to go on for a very long time for much longer, at any rate, than any of the previous ones Elsie, who was enjoying it immensely did not mind a scrap, and even before it had ended she was planning a little ruse which would ensure that she and Sam Adams had the next dance together Whiston had a different plan in mind for her he was determined that they would both of them leave as soon as the music stopped.

4   Make up a sentence about a couple dancing, and shape it in such a way that a dash is one of the punctuation marks you need.

5   Read the fourth paragraph again and notice how short the sentences are. Then write a paragraph of about 50 words describing a scene at a dance—or some other scene if you like—and include in it at least one very short sentence.

18 Dashes, used in pairs

Two dashes may be used to separate a word, or an expression, or even a whole statement, from the rest of the sentence. They form an enclosure round it:

The most beautiful feature of the English countryside—its greenness—would be missing entirely if we did not have so much rain and grey sky.

Some writers—one thinks of Wordsworth, for example, or Thomas Hardy—will always be associated with certain districts of England.

When dashes are used in pairs in this way, they are like brackets. But they are sometimes preferable, visually, to brackets, because they lead the eye through the sentence more smoothly.

Elsie went from the dancing-room to the card-room. After searching for a moment—the room was in a cloud of smoke—she found Whiston playing cribbage. Radiant, roused, animated, she went up to him and greeted him. She was too vibrant a note in the quiet room. He lifted his head, and a frown knitted his gloomy forehead.

'Are you playing cribbage? Is it exciting? How are you getting on?' she chattered.

He looked at her. None of these questions needed answering, and he did not feel in touch with her.

'I do wish you could dance,' she said.

'Well, I can't. So you enjoy yourself.'

'But I should enjoy it better if I could dance with you.'

'I'm not made that way,' he said.

'Then you ought to be!' she cried.

'Well, it's my fault, not yours. You enjoy yourself.'

---

1   Look at the second sentence. Why do you think Lawrence included the statement between the dashes?

2   In four of the following sentences a pair of dashes would have been better than the pair of commas that have been used. Write those four again, with the dashes put in:

Two mornings later, after discussing it quite calmly, they decided to try and make a fresh start.

Another suggestion of Elsie's rather a silly one, Whiston thought, was that they should stay away from each other for a whole week.

One of the rules in force at Sam Adams's warehouse, it was the strictest rule of all and was never broken, was that smoking was forbidden in the stock room.

Never in his whole life, as far as he could remember, had he felt so miserable as he did then.

He opened the door quietly, without knocking, and went into the room.

When Whiston spoke in that tone of voice, Elsie knew all the signs, it meant that his temper was nearing breaking-point.

She made up her mind, even though she knew she was doing wrong, to say nothing about it.

Suddenly, she had no idea what caused it, she felt an irresistible impulse to giggle.

3   In a paragraph of between 50 and 100 words describe a scene in a smoky games-room. The people might be playing cards, perhaps, or billiards, or table-tennis, or some other game. Try to include one expression or statement which is separate from the words that surround it and which needs to be enclosed between a pair of dashes.

19   Quoted speech

Elsie turned to the cribbage board. 'Are you white or red?' she asked Whiston.

'He's red,' replied his partner.

'Then you're losing,' she said, still to Whiston. And she lifted the red peg from the board.

'Put it back in its right place,' said Whiston.

'Where was it?' she asked gaily, knowing her transgression. He took the little red peg away from her and stuck it in its hole.

The cards were shuffled.

'What a shame you're losing!' said Elsie.

'You'd better cut for him,' said the partner.

She did so hastily. The cards were dealt. She put her hand on his shoulder, looking at his cards. It moved him more strongly than was comfortable, to have her hand on his shoulder, her curls dangling and touching his ears, whilst she was roused to another man. It made the blood flame over him.

At that moment Sam Adams appeared. . . .

If the quoted words are followed by a *he said*, or by some other expression of that kind, there are only three punctuation marks that can come at the end of them. It will be either a comma:

> *'Put it back in its right place,' said Whiston.*

Or a question mark:

> *'Where was it?' she asked.*

Or an exclamation mark:

> *'What a shame you're losing!' said Elsie.*

And no matter which one of the three it is, the *said* part always begins with a small letter.

We can also put the *said* part first. We put a comma after it—or sometimes a colon—and begin the quoted words with a capital letter:

> *Then the partner said, 'You'd better cut the cards.'*

1   Will you now punctuate this passage. Only the full stops and one exclamation mark have been put in. You will need commas, quotation marks, and a question mark. You will also need to change some of the capital letters to small ones, and some of the small ones to capitals.

Write the quotation marks extra clearly, and *space them properly*. The spacing should be the same as it is on page 40 with the quotation marks having spaces to themselves, and with the 'unquoting' ones put *after* the punctuation.

I think it's your turn to cut the cards said Whiston's partner.

Who's winning Asked Elsie.

Whiston took no notice. The man next to him dealt the cards and the game began. An ace of diamonds was turned up.

Snap! Shouted Elsie.

I think you'd better get back to the dance-floor said Whiston wearily.

Elsie bent down and whispered if you're really so keen to get rid of me I'll go and have another dance with Sam Adams.

That would be an excellent idea Said Whiston dryly.

2   Now continue the conversation (the one you have just punctuated) for about ten lines more. (Elsie might perhaps continue to bait Whiston until a row starts up . . . or Sam Adams might come in. . . .)

3   Improve the punctuation of these passages. You will need one colon and three dashes:

As soon as the music for the next dance began, it was a slow waltz, Sam Adams came striding across towards Elsie.

Elsie could see at a glance what was troubling Whiston, he was eaten up with jealousy.

The music sounded very sweet, sweeter, Elsie felt, than any music she had ever heard before in her whole life.

4   *She put her hand on his shoulder, looking at his cards,* That sentence consists of a main clause followed by a participle phrase. Without reversing the order in which the two acts that Elsie makes are mentioned, rewrite the sentences in such a way that the participle phrase comes first and the main clause second.

5   And now rewrite it in the form of two main clauses.

20 Putting *he said* in the middle of a quoted sentence

At that moment Sam Adams appeared, florid and boisterous, intoxicated more with himself, with the dancing, than with wine. In his eye the curious, impersonal light gleamed.

'I thought I should find you here, Elsie,' he cried.

'What made you think so?' she replied, the mischief rousing in her.

'It would never have occurred to me,' he said, 'to look for you among the ladies.'

He laughed, bowed, and offered her his arm. 'Madam, the music waits.'

She went forward with him to take her place at the dance. The music sounded. Everybody was ready. Adams stood with his body near her, exerting his attraction over her. She stooped for her pocket handkerchief, and shook it as she rose. It shook out and fell from her hand. With agony, she saw that she had taken out a white stocking instead of a handkerchief. For a second it lay on the floor, a twist of white stocking. Then, in an instant, Adams picked it up, with a little, surprised laugh of triumph.

'That'll do for me,' he whispered. And he stuffed the stocking in his trouser pocket, and quickly offered her his handkerchief.

The *said* part can come in the middle of a quoted sentence. Often it fits in there very neatly and unobtrusively:

'It would never have occurred to me,' he said, 'to look for you among the ladies.'

If you put it there you must be careful not to begin the second part of the quoted sentence with a capital letter, because doing that will break the continuity.

'It would never have occurred to me,' he said, 'To look for you among the ladies.'

The capital T destroys the continuity of Sam Adams's remark.

1   Re-arrange and re-punctuate each of these passages in such a way that the *said* part breaks into the quoted sentence:

'I'd feel very honoured if you'd come and have a drink with me after this dance,' he said.

He added, 'I suppose you realise that you're by far the prettiest girl in the room.'

'Surely, Elsie, you haven't forgotten your promise,' he whispered.

2   Here is a passage of quoted speech which is preceded by a statement about the speaker:

She lowered her voice and said, 'Whiston doesn't dance. He's not interested in that sort of thing.'

We will re-arrange it:

'Whiston doesn't dance,' she said, lowering her voice. 'He's not interested in that sort of thing.'

Will you now re-arrange each of these passages in the same way:

He swallowed down a gulp of beer and said, 'Wait a bit, Elsie! Yes, of course I remember.'

Elsie took his hand and said, 'I know you've been patient. You've been more patient than I've deserved.'

He put on a serious frown and asked, 'Would you mind awfully much, Elsie, if we didn't stay till the end of the dance?'

He flushed angrily and replied, 'There's only one thing to do and that's to break off our engagement.'

He got up and went towards the door and said, 'In that case I'll go home on my own.'

3   *He said . . . she said . . . Said,* used to the exclusion of all other words, becomes monotonous. In the extract Lawrence uses three other words instead of *said.* Write them down.

4   Now make up a conversation, about five lines long, which Sam Adams and Elsie have while they are dancing, and introduce into it some of your own variations on the word *said.* Remember to start a new paragraph every time you switch from one speaker to the other.

21   Paragraphing quoted speech

When the dance was over, Adams yielded her up. Whiston came to her.

'What was it you dropped?' Whiston asked.

'I thought it was my handkerchief,' she said. 'I'd taken a stocking by mistake.'

'And he's got it?'

'Yes.'

'Are you going to let him keep it?'

There was a long pause.

Whiston's face flushed, and his blue eyes went hard with opposition. 'Am I to go and have it out with him?' he asked.

'No,' she said, pale. 'I don't want you to say anything about it.'

He sat exasperated and nonplussed. 'You'll let him keep it then?'

She sat silent and made no form of answer.

He started up. 'What do you mean by it?' he said, dark with fury. 'I'm not stopping here. Are you coming with me?'

She rose mutely, and they went out of the room. Adams had not noticed. In a few moments they were in the street.

Will you look now at the paragraphing of that passage.

Notice, first, that a new paragraph begins every time there is a switch from one speaker to the other. It doesn't matter how short the paragraph turns out to be. One of them consists of only one word.

Next, notice that sometimes the new paragraph may begin with a brief *comment* about the speaker, instead of with the quoted words. Three paragraphs in the extract begin like that.

And lastly notice that often the paragraphing by itself is enough to show which person is speaking. So there is no need to say who it is every time. If you remember this you can get rid of a lot of boring *he said*s.

1   Make up a conversation held at table during the evening
meal, between two people, about some incident that took
place that day. Let it be roughly half a page long, and take
particular care over the paragraphing.

From time to time, when you are writing it, glance at
some of the passages of conversation that we have quoted
from Lawrence's writing, and notice the various ways in
which he introduces the speeches. Try to introduce yours
in an equally varied way. For example, you might sometimes
begin a paragraph with a comment about the person who is
about to speak.

2   Now make up another conversation, of about the same
length as your previous one, between at least three people—
at a party, perhaps, or in a bus queue, or waiting for a train,
or in any other situation you like to think of. This time try to
include some paragraphs that consist only of the spoken
words, like the fourth, fifth and sixth paragraphs in the
extract. Remember that occasionally you can show who is
speaking by making the speakers address each other by
name:

'Are you ready, Con?'
'Yes, Lucy, when you are.'
'Then I think we'd better go.'

'What the hell do you mean?' he said, in a black fury.
She went at his side, in silence, neutral.
'The great hog!' he added.
Then they went a long time in silence through the frozen, deserted darkness of the town. She felt she could not go indoors. They were drawing near her house.
'I don't want to go home,' she suddenly cried in distress and anguish.
He looked at her. 'Why don't you?' he said.
'I don't!' she sobbed.
He heard somebody coming.
'Well, we can walk a bit farther,' he said.
He held her by the arm. They could not speak.
'What's the matter?' he asked at length.

People sometimes use exclamation marks to draw the reader's attention to the fact that he has just read something humorous:

As soon as she stepped onto the ice she fell flat on her face!

'Isn't that funny?' says the exclamation mark. It's not usually a good idea to use them in that way. If something is to be funny the humour must have its own strength: it's no good *telling* the reader it's funny.

People sometimes use them, too, to mean 'Isn't that amazing?':

It is said that the universe contains more than a hundred thousand million stars!

That isn't a good idea either. If something is amazing, let it speak for itself.

It's usually best to reserve exclamation marks for what they are meant for—that is, for marking words that are expressed with strong emotion:

'You idiot!' he yelled.
'I don't!' she sobbed.
'No!' he shouted.

1   What is the effect of the exclamation mark in the third paragraph?

2   Improve the punctuation of this passage. One of the full stops should be an exclamation mark; two of the commas should be dashes; and two commas are missing:

It was the first time they had quarrelled. Nor, Whiston reflected, as they walked forward in silence would it be likely to be the last. What a dreadful evening it had been. He found himself sinking into a mood of despair. Elsie on the other hand, seemed quite buoyed up. He glanced at her. Suddenly it occurred to him, and his heart sank as he realised what he was thinking, that there were certain features in her character that he despised.

3   Make up a conversation, about half a page long, in which a boy and a girl have a quarrel on their way home after an evening out together. You can, if you want to, introduce short passages of narrative into it—to explain how they were travelling, perhaps, or where they were, or what the weather was like. Remember to start a new paragraph every time the attention is switched from one speaker to the other. And try to present the conversation in an interesting way. For example, you might sometimes begin a paragraph with a comment about the speaker; or you might have some paragraphs which consist of the quoted words only, without any *he said*.

23   Apostrophes

If we put an *'s* onto the end of a noun we express an *of*:

Whiston was a miner's son.

If the noun already ends with an *s* because it is in the plural, we do not put an *'s* after it but only an apostrophe:

The miners' cottages were cramped and ugly.

There is just one exception: for *of it* we write *its*—not *it's*:

Whiston hated the town. He detested its grey, dingy streets and its ugly houses.

Apostrophes also serve the quite different purpose of showing that we have left out a letter, or sometimes two or three letters. We use them to reproduce the abbreviations of speech. *It's* stands of *it is*, *don't* for *do not*, *won't* for *will not*, and so on.

Every apostrophe must have a space to itself—in handwriting as well as in print.

'. . . What's the matter?' he asked at length, puzzled.

She began to cry again. At last he took her in his arms to soothe her. She sobbed by herself, almost unaware of him.

'Tell me what's the matter, Elsie,' he said.

He kissed the girl's wet face and caressed her. She made no response. He was puzzled and tender and miserable. At length she became quiet. Then he kissed her, and she put her arms round him, and clung to him very tight, as if for fear and anguish. He held her in his arms, wondering. He held her very safe, and his heart was white-hot with love for her. His mind was amazed. He could only hold her against his chest that was white-hot with love and belief in her. So she was restored at last.

---

1   Explain the meaning of the apostrophe in the first line. . .

2   . . . and of the one in the fifth line.

3   Make up a sentence in which the word *girl's* is used, with the apostrophe expressing the omission of a letter.

4   Now make up a sentence, or a short passage, with the word *girls'* in it, and do it in such a way that this word could not be mistaken, even when only heard (and not seen on the page) for *girl's*.

5   Make up a sentence which has both *it's* and *its* in it.

6   Rewrite these sentences correctly:
  'What we both need,' said Elsie, 'is a good nights rest.'
  He said he would come and see her again in a few weeks time.

7   Make up two sentences about a bad-tempered person, in such a way that you can put a colon after the first one. If you want some help turn back to page 32.

8   And now make up a sentence, with a dash in it, about a conceited person. Turn back to page 36 if you want help.

9   Look at the extract again and notice how short and final the last sentence is. It brings the paragraph to a firm close. Then write a paragraph, of between five and ten lines, describing a boy saying goodbye to a girl on a station platform, and try to give it an equally firm ending.

Choosing words

Extracts taken from

Daphne du Maurier:
The Birds

The exercises that follow include many revision questions, about matters that were dealt with in earlier sections of the book.

24 Adjectives

Awful, nice, lovely, ghastly, terrible, terrific, fantastic, marvellous—adjectives like these are among the most overworked words in the language. They have become easy, lazy words, to be applied without thought to everything under the sun. In speech, no one minds; but in writing they are very feeble. So it is usually best to avoid them.

Sometimes, too, try to do better than the obvious general adjective. Instead of telling your reader that something is *good*, or *bad*, try to think of an adjective that will tell him in what way it is one or other of these. For example: *A good speech. Good* can be applied to all kinds of different things—health, the weather, a person, a meal. . . . *A thoughtful speech. Thoughtful* can't. Its range is narrower. For this reason it tells us more about the speech than *good* does.

Here are some more examples—in pairs, with the general adjective first and the sharper one second.

A good foundation . . . a firm foundation. A good judge of character . . . a shrewd judge of character. A bad handicap . . . a severe handicap. A bad decline in living standards . . . a sharp decline. Horrible colours . . . crude colours. A great disappointment . . . a bitter disappointment. An awful liar . . . a confirmed liar.

On December the third the wind changed and it was winter. Until then the autumn had been mellow, soft. The leaves had lingered on the trees, golden red, and the hedgerows were still green. The earth was rich where the plough had turned it. It was that night the weather turned. Nat's bedroom faced east. He woke just after two and heard the wind in the chimney—the east wind, cold and dry. It sounded hollow in the chimney, and a loose slate rattled on the roof. Nat listened, and he could hear the sea roaring in the bay. Even the air in the small bedroom had turned chill. A draught came under the skirting of the door, blowing upon the bed. Nat drew the blanket round him, leant closer to the back of his sleeping wife, and stayed wakeful, watchful, aware of misgiving without cause.

Then he heard the tapping on the window. . . .

---

1   In that passage the adjectives are simple and precise:
mellow, soft, green, cold, dry, chill. . . . In the following
sentences they are generalised and vague:

Later that evening there was a terrific *sunset.*

In this chapter there is a marvellous *description of the frost.*

From this window we had a nice *view of the sea.*

Some of the roads were so awful *that we found it impossible to
drive along them.*

The trees were clothed in the wonderful *colours of autumn.*

He was a fantastic *swimmer.*

In each of those sentences choose a more precise adjective
than the one that has been used. Write the sentences out in
full, with your adjectives in them.

2   What kind of phrase is *blowing upon the bed,* in line 11?
If you can't answer search among the earlier sections of this
book.

3   What noun is the phrase associated with?

4   *Sitting up in bed a strange sound fell upon Nat's ears.*
What noun is the phrase *sitting up in bed* associated with in
that sentence? Rewrite the sentence in such a way as to get
rid of the muddle.

5   Improve this passage by choosing adjectives that are
more precise than those that have been used. Write the
passage out in full, with the improvements put in:

The mist was much worse *on the lower slopes of the mountain.
Gradually, as they trudged on, the two boys began to realise
what an* awful *situation they were in. The darkness was closing
round them, and there were no* decent *paths—only sheep-
tracks. Soon, they knew, the temperature would fall further
and the cold would become* very great.

6   Imagine that Nat wakes up not on the cold night that
Daphne du Maurier describes, but on a warm summer's
night. Describe the scene in a paragraph of about the same
length as that second one of hers, and let your aim be the
same as hers—that is, to create the atmosphere of the scene,
rather than to make something happen. Let any adjectives
you introduce be as simple and precise as hers are.

25 Nouns

Thing is not always a bad word, but sometimes it hides a poverty of vocabulary. It will usually seem bad in writing if you use it simply in order to save yourself the trouble of thinking of the right noun. Try to think of the *name* of the thing you are writing about, and use that instead.

One of the most popular things on the television . . .
(programmes)

An important place in the school timetable has always been given to things like history and literature. (subjects)

The Board of Film Censors is a completely unnecessary thing. (institution)

These things all take place in the early chapters of the book. (events)

Greed is a basic human thing. (instinct)

Then he heard the tapping on the window. There was no creeper on the cottage walls to break loose and scratch upon the pane. He listened, and the tapping continued until, irritated by the sound, Nat got out of bed and went to the window. He opened it, and as he did so something brushed his hand, jabbing at his knuckles, grazing the skin. Then he saw the flutter of the wings and it was gone, over the roof, behind the cottage.

It was a bird. What kind of bird he could not tell. The wind must have driven it to shelter on the sill.

He shut the window and went back to bed, but feeling his knuckles wet he put his mouth to the scratch. The bird had drawn blood. Frightened, he supposed, and bewildered, the bird, seeking shelter, had stabbed at him in the darkness. Once more he settled himself to sleep.

Presently the tapping came again. . . .

---

1   Improve these sentences by using a more precise noun than *thing*:

One very exciting thing in this story is the discovery of the hidden documents.

To be lost on these moors is a frightening thing.

Two things I enjoy a great deal are riding and sailing.

This valley, seen from the slopes of the mountain, is one of the most beautiful things in the world.

2   Improve this passage by choosing adjectives that are more precise. Write the passage out in full, with the improvements put in:

It was a lovely *autumn evening. A* nice *breeze drifted in from the sea, stirring the reeds in the estuary. The sun was going down, and its rays laid a path of* marvellous *light across the water. A flight of geese went speeding westward. They were a* fantastic *sight. The thrust of their heads and necks seemed to express a* terrific *eagerness to reach their destination.*

3   What kind of phrase is *irritated by the sound,* in line 4? If you can't answer search among the earlier sections of this book.

4   What noun is the phrase associated with?

5   Make up a sentence in which the word *irritated* is used not as part of a phrase but as the main verb of a sentence.

6   *A bird tapping on the window.* That is not a complete sentence. Turn it into one by altering the second syllable of '*tapping*'.

7   Now turn it into a complete sentence by adding a word in front of *tapping*. If you can't, turn back to Section 2.

8   And now turn it into one by adding two words in front of *tapping*.

9   Daphne du Maurier wrote (in the second paragraph): *The wind must have driven it . . .* not: *The wind had driven it . . .* Explain the difference.

26　*Got**

Got is not always a bad word. And it is certainly not bad just because it comes naturally. Nothing could be more mistaken than the view that to write well you have to write stiffly and formally.

He got very angry.　The garden had got out of hand.　I've got to finish this by tomorrow.　I got this book from the library.

Does *got* seem bad in any of those sentences? Surely not. But it does in some. Does it, do you think, in any of these?

As the evening got nearer . . . (drew)　The composer got this effect by using a full orchestra. (achieved)　After a few days he got malarial fever. (caught)

Often, too, in writing, when *got* is put in after a possessive *have* or *had*, it jars:

Her room had got a window looking out over the sea.　This song has got a beautiful rhythm.　Some animals have got a way of understanding what people say.

If you read those sentences again, without the *got*s, you will see the improvement.

Presently the tapping came again, this time more forceful, more insistent, and now his wife woke at the sound, and turning in the bed said to him, 'See to the window, Nat; it's rattling.'

He went to the window for the second time. Now, when he opened it, there was not one bird on the sill but half a dozen. They flew straight into his face, attacking him. He shouted, striking out at them with his arms, scattering them. Like the first one, they flew over the roof and disappeared. Quickly he let the window fall and latched it.

'Did you hear that?' he said. 'They went for me. Tried to peck my eyes.' He stood by the window, peering into the night. His wife, heavy with sleep, murmured from the bed.

'I'm not making it up,' he said, angry at her suggestion.

Suddenly a frightened cry came from the room across the passage where the children slept.

---

*Got is of course part of the verb *to get*, and much of what is said here applies to *get* as well.

1   Replace *got* in these sentences with a better word:

The storm got gradually nearer.

Towards the end of his life he got very famous.

His heroic behaviour got the admiration of everyone.

2   Quote the subordinate clause that comes in the second sentence of the second paragraph. (Turn back to Section 4 if you need help.) Then quote the one that comes in the last sentence of the passage.

3   What does the apostrophe stand for in line 3? Make up a sentence with *its* in it.

4   Too much has been crowded into this next sentence. Rewrite it, making three sentences of it.

It was a cold December day, and there was no wind and the earth was as hard as iron, so that Nat's boots, as he climbed the cliff path, struck sharply against the ridges of frozen mud.

5   Now divide this one into three:

Nat listened, and the tapping continued, and he got out of bed and went to the window.

6   Read the second paragraph of the extract again and notice how clear-cut the sentences are. Most of them are fairly short: there are six full stops in five lines. In a few sentences, that are equally clear and short, describe what Nat might have seen, or heard, as he stood by the window *peering into the night* (line 12). Write your description in such a way that it would fit into Daphne du Maurier's book at this point.

7   Rewrite this passage in such a way that all the sentences are complete:

The mild autumn weather continued. Not a trace of mist or cold. On either side of the lane the hedgerows were still green, and the ploughed earth lay rich and soft. The leaves still lingering on the trees. Nat, tramping home across the fields, saw the gulls wheeling above the tractor. So many of them that from time to time they hid it completely. He paused to watch the whirling cloud of whiteness. This being a sight that never failed to fascinate him.

27 *Lot* and *bit*

These words slip so easily and naturally into our speech that we have to be extra careful over them when we are writing.

Lot doesn't always sound bad in writing; but it does sometimes. When does it? It's not easy to say. In the end, I think, one would have to admit that only the ear can decide.

I liked this book a lot. . . . I liked this book very much.
He has lots more patience than most people. . . . He has much more patience, far more patience.

If you don't feel confident enough to decide, why not avoid *lot* altogether? But if you do use it, never put *got* in front of it, because when these two words are put down together in writing they made a childish jingle:

He has got a lot of . . .
Bit sometimes jars, in writing:
There is one very funny bit in this book. . . . one very funny passage.   A good bit more expensive. . . . much more expensive.   After a bit. . . . after a while.

There came a second cry of terror, this time from both children, and stumbling into their room Nat felt the beating of wings about him in the darkness. The window was wide open. Through it came the birds, hitting first the ceiling and the walls, then swerving in mid-flight, and turning to the children in their beds.

'It's all right, I'm here,' shouted Nat, and the children flung themselves, screaming, upon him, while in the darkness the birds rose and dived and came for him again. Swiftly he pushed the children through the door to the passage and shut it upon them, so that he was alone now, in their bedroom, with the birds.

---

1   Rewrite these sentences without using *lot*:

The garden has got a lot of nettles in it.

There was a lot of sadness in her heart.

This library has got a lot of valuable books in it.
Some of these schools are a lot too big.

2   Now rewrite these sentences, using a better word than
bit:

One bit in this play was especially dramatic.
This bit of the garden was quite free of weeds.
I remember one bit in my dream very clearly.

3   In the following passage four of the commas are wrong.
One should be a full stop, one a colon, and two should be
dashes. Write the passage out, putting these four mistakes
right:

*Nat had one trait of character that set him apart from the other
villagers, he was a solitary man. He often went for walks by
himself, he was much happier going on his own than with his
children, even though he was a devoted father. His favourite
walk, he must have done it a thousand times, he reckoned, was
across the meadows at the far end of the village and back
through the woods.*

4   Improve this passage by choosing better adjectives. Write
the passage out in full, with the improvements put in:

The view from the top of these cliffs is terrific. *To the west, on
a nice day, you can see the headlands stretching away into the
distance. In front, and below, lies the* wonderful *floor of the
ocean. But to the east the beauty of the scene is marred by a*
horrible *caravan site, which covers the hillside.*

5   Without looking at the next page, write a short
paragraph (perhaps five or six lines long) which will carry the
story forward from the point it has reached at the end of the
passage on the opposite page.

28 *Definitely* and *really*

In conversation we often use *definitely* as a word of general emphasis, meaning *certainly* or *decidedly*. *You definitely ought to give that job up.* But that is not the true meaning of *definitely*, and in writing it is better not to use it in that way. This is not just some fussy old-fashioned rule.
Conversational *definitelys*, used purely for emphasis, nearly always spoil a sentence:
Rebecca is definitely a novel of great sadness and beauty.
Nowadays many people definitely get married too young.
I definitely believe that everyone should be concerned with the preservation of wild-life.

If you read those sentences again, leaving out the *definitelys*. you will see the improvement.

Really means *in reality*. But in speech we often use it instead of words like *very* or *certainly,* and this habit can easily spread into our writing. It is better not to let it.
The journey really was tiring. . . . The journey was very tiring. This really is an interesting play. . . . This is certainly an interesting play. I really did enjoy it. . . . I enjoyed it immensely.

He seized a blanket from the nearest bed, and using it as a weapon flung it to the right and left about him in the air. He felt the thud of bodies, heard the fluttering of wings, but they were not yet defeated, for again and again they returned to the assault, jabbing his hands, his head, the little stabbing beaks sharp as a pointed fork. The blanket became a weapon of defence: he wound it about his head. Then in greater darkness he beat at the birds with his bare hands. He dared not stumble to the door and open it, lest in doing so the birds should follow him.

At last the beating of the wings about him lessened and then withdrew. He waited, listened. There was no sound except the fretful crying of one of the children from the bedroom beyond. The fluttering, the whirring of the wings had ceased.

---

1   Here is a description of an empty house, written in poor English. Some of the sentences are incomplete, and some of the words are badly chosen. Rewrite it in better English, without altering the meaning:

The house was in an awful state. A lot worse than I expected. I stood in the front room, and what I saw made me feel really bad. Not a single bit of furniture left in it, and the light switches had been torn from their sockets. Old newspapers and cigarette stubs lying about on the floor. Quite a bit of dampness, too, had got through the wall beneath the window, and the moisture had got nearly half-way across the floorboards. Definitely a depressing sight.

2   Why is there a colon in line 7 of the extract? If you can't explain why, look back to Section 15.

3   In one of the following passages a colon is better than the full stop that has been used. Write that one out again, with the colon put in:

The children flung themselves on their father, screaming with fright. He bundled them out of the door into the passage.

The birds attacked him from all sides. Their beaks were as sharp as pointed forks.

But in his hurry he made one mistake. He forgot to lock the door.

4   Make up two sentences (about Nat, or the children, or the birds) and write them in such a way that the second one explains the first one, or completes the sense of it—so that you need to put a colon after the first one.

5   Write a passage of conversation (about ten lines long) which could form a continuation of the extract quoted on the opposite page. Begin a new paragraph with these words: *After a moment he heard his wife's footsteps in the passage. She banged on the door.* Then continue with the conversation that she and Nat have. Remember to start a new paragraph every time there is a switch from one speaker to the other. Remember, too, that often the paragraphing by itself is enough to show which person is speaking; so there will be no need for a *he said* or *she said* every time.

Slang can be very effective in writing. But it must be used sparingly, and with judgement. A good writer will introduce a piece of slang, or an everyday expression, to achieve a contrast—to bring some light relief into his writing perhaps, or to give it a touch of down-to-earth vigour. And in order not to blunt the contrasts which this kind of language makes possible, he uses it only occasionally.

That sort of writer is the very opposite of someone who uses casual, everyday expressions all the time, without thought—who uses them not deliberately, to make a contrast, but because they are the first words that come to his mind. That gives a very bad impression. It reduces his writing to the level of slovenly chat.

Never use a slang phrase or a chatty expression thoughtlessly. Whenever you find that you are about to, be aware of what you are doing, and ask yourself if you are gaining anything by using it. If you are not, if you are choosing it merely because it is saving you the trouble of writing more carefully, don't use it. Instead, translate it into clear, simple English.

Nat stared about him. The cold grey morning light exposed the room. The dead lay on the floor. He gazed at the little corpses, shocked and horrified. They were all small birds, none of any size. There must have been fifty of them lying there upon the floor. There were robins, finches, sparrows, blue tits, larks and bramblings. Some had lost feathers in the fight; others had blood—his blood—upon their beaks.

Sickened, Nat went to the window and stared out across his patch of garden to the fields. It was bitter cold, and the ground had all the hard black look of frost—not white frost, to shine in the morning sun, but the black frost that the east wind brings. The sea, fiercer now with the turning tide, white-capped and steep, broke harshly in the bay. Of the birds there was no sign. There was no sound at all but the east wind and the sea.

---

1   This next passage is very chatty and casual, and some of the adjectives are badly chosen. Rewrite it in better English, keeping the meaning the same:

The grounds of Kendall House are absolutely fantastic. What sticks in my mind most is the view from the terrace. The marvellous thing about this view is the stretch of water that can be seen way off in the distance. In actual fact it's only a pond, but it has been really cleverly placed, so that when you see it from the terrace you are kidded into thinking it's a bit of real river. It's even got a faked up bridge over it. Every single thing in these grounds has definitely been put there for a purpose. For example, on one side there are a whole lot of dark trees, almost like a wood really, and they add a bit of mystery to what would otherwise be a very open view.

2   Write down the main verbs of the first five sentences of the quoted extract (five words).

3   In the extract there are two occasions on which the writer is repetitive—that is to say, on each occasion the same idea is expressed twice (though of course in a different form). Quote these two examples of repetition.

4   Look at the pair of dashes in line 7 and satisfy yourself that you understand the purpose of them. Then make up a sentence (perhaps about the birds, or about Nat) in such a way that you need to use a pair of dashes in it.

5   Will you now turn back to page 52 and look at the quoted passage. Imagine that you are writing the story, and that you have completed that passage and are about to continue with a third paragraph. You have already written the first sentence of it (*Then he heard the tapping on the window*). Continue it, and complete it, in such a way as to take the story along a different line from that taken by Daphne du Maurier's, with the tapping being caused by something other than birds (a ghost? . . . a burglar? . . .) Let your paragraph be about half a page long.

Ways of going wrong

Extracts taken from

Graham Greene:
The Power and the Glory

The exercises that follow include many revision questions, about matters that were dealt with in earlier sections of the book.

30 *Is when*

A democratic country is when the people elect the government.

When always refers to time. We say that something *happens* when. *It started to rain when I left the house.* We can never say that something *is* when. No 'thing'—whether it be a democratic country or anything else—can be a period of time. The sentence should read:

A democratic country is one in which the people elect the government.

Here is another badly written sentence:

An unexpected difficulty was when he tried to push the boat out into the water.

An unexpected difficulty can't be a time when somebody did something. What the writer meant was:

An unexpected difficulty arose *when he tried to push the boat out into the water.*

Is when is a treacherous phrase. It is nearly always wrong.

In these extracts from *The Power and the Glory*, by Graham Greene. The Mexican authorities are searching for the village priest, who is disguised as a peasant. If he is caught he will be shot. He has just celebrated Mass.

Somebody opened the door. A voice whispered urgently, 'They're here.' Through the door the world was faintly visible, and a cock in the village crowed.

Maria said, 'Come to the hut quickly. They are all round the village.'

He followed the woman, scurrying across the village to her hut. There was no sign of the police—only the grey morning, and the chickens and turkeys astir, flopping down from the trees in which they had roosted during the night.

Maria plucked at him. 'Get in quick. On to the bed. Let me smell your breath. O God, anyone can tell . . . wine. . . .'

Suddenly, out of the forest, a hundred yards away, an officer rode. In the absolute stillness you could hear the creaking of his revolver holster as he turned and waved.

---

1   Improve this sentence:

The first idea the villagers had that the police were in the area was when a lieutenant came riding out of the forest soon after the dawn had broken followed by three or four men carrying rifles at the trail.

Re-shape it as much as you like. You might decide, for example, to divide it into two or even three sentences, or to change some of the words. But you mustn't alter the meaning.

2   And now improve this one:

The most exciting passage in Graham Greene's novel is when he describes the hunt for the priest.

3   Re-arrange the second paragraph of the quoted passage in such a way that *Maria said* comes between the two sentences she speaks.

4   Rewrite this passage in the form of four complete sentences:

A tense moment. The service just over. The villagers emerging from the little church, talking quietly among themselves. Not knowing that the police were waiting just out of sight round the corner.

5   Quote, from the extract, two participle phrases, and say what noun—or nouns—each one goes with. If you need help turn to page 12.

6   Graham Greene describes an exciting scene. The details he introduces (the cock, the creaking of the holster, the birds flopping down from the trees) make it seem intensely real; and the short sentences heighten the sense of drama. Using both these means (sharp detail and short sentences) describe a tense scene of some other kind—in a city street late at night perhaps . . . or in an empty house. . . . Let your description be about five to ten lines long.

31   Switching tenses

The sun was setting, and the mist was closing in upon us. For the last time (because now we had reached the end of our holiday) we clean out the tents and round up the dogs. We are going to travel by night. We knew that if we went by day the dogs would suffer from the heat.

The switches of tense spoil that piece of writing. They irritate because they are unconsidered and accidental.

Usually, when we are describing something that happened in the past, we use the past tense. We *can* use the present. Using the present tense to describe past events is a literary device. It is only used occasionally, and its purpose is to make the events seem more immediate and dramatic. But whether we use the present or the past, we must be consistent and keep to one or the other.

Will you now rewrite the passage we have just quoted, putting it all in the past tense. And when you have done that write it out again in the present tense (with the idea, possibly, of making it seem more dramatic).

All round the little clearing the police appeared. They must have marched very quickly, for only the officer had a horse. Rifles at the trail, they approached the small group of huts. One man had a puttee* trailing behind him: it had probably caught on something in the forest. He tripped on it and fell with a great clatter of cartridge belt on gunstock. The lieutenant on the horse looked round and then turned his bitter and angry face upon the silent huts.

The woman was pulling at the priest from inside the hut. She said, 'Bite this. Quick.' He came into the dusk of the room. She had a small raw onion in her hand. 'Bite it,' she said. He bit it and began to weep. He could hear the pad, pad of the cautious horse hoofs advancing between the huts.

'Give it to me.' She made it disappear somewhere into her clothes: it was a trick all women seemed to know. 'Get on to the bed.'

But before he could move a horse blocked the doorway. . . .

---

*a long band of cloth wound round the leg for protection

1   Rewrite this passage in the past tense:

He follows the woman, scurrying across the village to her hut. There is no sign of the police—only the grey morning, and the chickens and turkeys astir, flopping down from the trees in which they have roosted during the night.

When you have finished, turn back to page 66 and look at the third paragraph of the extract.

2   Will you now put these passages right:

The priest hurried into the hut and lies down on the bed. Several minutes passed, but there is still no sign of the police. He waits there, in an agony of suspense.

The police had reached the village sooner than expected, and no one was able to hide.

The word soon went round the village that the search for the priest has begun.

All round the little clearing the police appeared. Rifles at the trail, they approach the small group of huts.

Maria's great fear was that the officer will smell the wine on the priest's breath. She picks up an onion and thrusts it in his mouth. 'Bite this!' she whispered.

3   Why is there a colon between the fourth and fifth sentences in the first paragraph of the extract?

4   And why is there one between the second and third sentences in the last paragraph but one?

5   The last line of the passage reads: *But before he could move a horse blocked the doorway.* Try to picture what Maria and the priest might have seen of the horse and its rider at this moment, as it *blocked the doorway*; and in two or three sentences describe what they saw. Try to introduce some sharp visual detail. When you have finished look at the first few sentences of the extract on page 70.

32   Forgetting to use pronouns

Pronouns are words like *I, you, he, him, her, it, they, them,* and we use them instead of nouns so as not to have to repeat ourselves unnecessarily. They can also take the form of adjectives, like *my, his, your, their.* Often, instead of using a pronoun, a person will name the noun again—even though he has only just mentioned it. There is no surer way of spoiling a sentence.

After a while we began to wonder what had happened to the team leader. Someone suggested that a search party should be sent out to search for the team leader.

Pronouns are excellent words. They give writing an air of neatness and economy. They help sentences to flow lightly and effortlessly. You should use them as often as you can.

Graham Greene wrote The Power and the Glory *shortly before the second world war.* The Power and the Glory *is probably Graham Greene's best novel. . . . It is probably his best novel.*

Some musicians despise guitars. These musicians think anyone can play guitars. . . . They think anyone can play them.

Graham Sutherland wanted to portray Churchill as a powerful figure, but instead Graham Sutherland made Churchill look arrogant . . . but instead he made him look arrogant.

. . . But before he could move a horse blocked the doorway. They could see a leg in riding-boots piped with scarlet; brass fittings gleamed; a hand in a glove rested on the high pommel. A voice cried, 'Come on out, all of you.' The horse stamped and a little pillar of dust went up. 'Come on out, I said.' Somewhere a shot was fired. The priest left the hut.

The dawn had broken: light feathers of colour were blown up the sky. A man still held his gun pointed upwards. A little ballon of grey smoke hung at the muzzle.

Out of all the huts the villagers were reluctantly emerging. The children were inquisitive and unfrightened. The men and women had the air already of people condemned by authority. None of them looked at the priest. They stared at the ground and waited.

---

1   Rewrite these passages, using the nouns in Roman type only once, when they are first mentioned, and using pronouns instead whenever they are mentioned again:

Suddenly an officer *rode out of the forest. In the stillness you could hear the swish of the officer's* baton *as the officer waved the baton in the air.*

Maria *had a raw* onion *in her hand. Maria thrust the onion at the* priest. *'Bite the onion,' Maria whispered.*
The priest bit the onion and began to weep. 'The onion tastes horrible,' the priest said.

The soldier *walked up to the* priest. *Without any warning the soldier grabbed the priest by the hair, pulled the priest forward, and told the priest to breathe out. 'Let me see if you smell of wine!' the soldier shouted.*

Maria *and the* priest *did not want the little* girl *to go near the* lieutenant, *but before Maria and the priest could stop her the girl stepped forward and stood by the lieutenant's* horse. *After a moment the girl lifted her hand and touched the horse's flank.*

2   Rewrite this passage in the form of five complete sentences. The first one is already complete:

It was a strange situation. The village looking as quiet and peaceful as ever. The peasants going about their daily tasks, seemingly unconcerned. No sign of the police. Yet a feeling of tension filling the air, as though some catastrophe were about to take place.

3   The semicolons between the second, third and fourth sentences of the extract show that the ideas expressed in these sentences are closely connected. Write a short passage describing a scene glimpsed through a window. Begin it with this sentence: *He glanced out of the window.* Then go on to complete it by adding three or four more sentences, which are separated from each other by semicolons because the ideas they express are closely connected.

4   Read again the last paragraph of the extract. Add a few sentences to the end of it and describe—from your imagination—two or three individuals among that group of people. Try to include some sharp detail (some slight movement that one of them made . . . the clothes that another was wearing. . . .) Try to keep your sentences as clear and simple as Graham Greene's, so that they follow on naturally after his.

33 Using *this* wrongly

The priest's breath smelt strongly of wine. This worried Maria to the point of distraction.

The *this* in that sentence is perfectly clear and correct, because the reader knows at once what it refers to. It refers to the fact that the priest's breath smelt of wine.

The ordinary policemen were all on foot. Only the officer had a horse. It was a fine white one, and as he rode forward he waved his revolver. This surprised the villagers, for they had been warned to expect mounted police.

In that sentence the *this* is not clear at all. For a moment the reader is completely misled.

Whenever you use a *this*, by itself, at the beginning of a statement, make sure that it doesn't leave your reader in a muddle, even for a moment.

The lieutenant said, 'Search the huts.' Time passed very slowly. Some pigs came grunting out of a hut, and a turkey-cock paced with evil dignity into the centre of the circle, puffing out its dusty feathers and tossing the long pink membrane from its beak. A soldier came up to the lieutenant and saluted sketchily. He said, 'They're all here.'

The lieutenant barked out, 'Attention. All of you. Listen to me.' The outer ring of police closed in, pushing the villagers together into a small group in front of the lieutenant. Only the children were left free. The priest saw his own child standing close to the lieutenant's horse. She could just reach above his boot. She put up her hand and touched the leather.

The lieutenant said, 'I am looking for . . . a priest.' He raised his voice: 'You know what that means—a traitor to the republic. Anyone who shelters him is a traitor too.'

The child had her hand on his boot. The police leant on their guns. One of them yawned. The turkey-cock went hissing back towards the hut.

The lieutenant said, 'If you've seen this priest, speak up. There's a reward of seven hundred pesos.'

Nobody spoke.

---

1   In three of the following passages the second of the two sentences begins badly. Rewrite those three sentences more clearly:

The police then herded the villagers into the church. This was their usual practice when they were searching for a suspect.

The lieutenant gave a cry of anger and lowered his hand to his revolver. This was so loud that it made the little girl jerk her head up in fear.

The child put up her hand and touched the leather of the lieutenant's boot with the tip of her finger. This caught his attention, and he looked down at her and smiled.

The police leant on their guns and yawned in a very obvious manner. This was their way of hinting to the lieutenant that his interrogation of the villagers had gone on long enough.

Slowly and off-handedly the lieutenant drew a silver case from his pocket and took out a small cigar. This suggested that he was in no hurry and that he meant to get the truth out of the villagers even if it took him all day.

2   Now look at the example given on the opposite page (beginning *The ordinary policemen were all on foot. . . .*) and rewrite it with the sentences in a different order. Re-arrange the order in such a way that the *This . . .* is no longer confusing. Don't alter any of the words.

3   Rewrite this passage in such a way as to put right the mistakes in the use of tenses:

One by one the villagers came out of the huts. Some of them stroll out slowly, to show that they have no fear of the police; others came scurrying out with frightened faces. Only the children are genuinely free of fear.

4   Graham Greene is not afraid to write short sentences, and you should not be, either. Notice, for example, how short they are in the last paragraph but two, and how short the last sentence of all is. In sentences as short as these—or nearly as short—write a brief description of some scene in which people are waiting in a state of tension for something to happen.

We use *like* to compare one thing to another. It must always
lead to a noun. *The moon is like a lamp.* If we put an
expression containing a verb after it, we get this kind of
language: . . . *like you do when you are tired.* To speak in
that way is very natural, but in writing it doesn't give a good
impression.

*It turned out just like I hoped it would.   They spoke to her
like they were dealing with a child.   I tried to picture the
village like it used to be, before the road had been built.   He
looked at me strangely, like he didn't know who I was.*

In some of those sentences, you will notice, the *like* would
seem bad even in speech. In writing it is bad in all of them:
the writer should have used *as* or *as if* or *as though*. Will you
write them out again, and make that alteration.

The lieutenant yanked his horse's head round towards them.
He said, 'Come up—one after the other—and let me have
your names. No, not the women—the men.'

They filed sullenly up and he questioned them: 'What's
your name? What do you do? Married? Which is your wife?
Have you heard of this priest?'

Only one man now stood between the priest and the
horse's head. The priest recited an act of contrition silently
with only half a mind. He was alone in front of the
lieutenant.

'Your name?'

'Montez.'

'Have you ever seen the priest?'

'No.'

'What do you do?'

'I have a little land.'

'Are you married?'

'Yes.'

'Which is your wife?'

Maria suddenly broke out, 'I'm his wife. Why do you
want to ask so many questions? Do you think he *looks* like a
priest?'

---

1   *Do you think he looks like a priest?* That *like* is right because it leads to a noun. *He did not behave like a priest should.* That one is wrong because it leads not to a noun but to an expression with a verb in it. Will you rewrite the sentence and correct the mistake.

2   Explain the meaning of the apostrophe in the first line of the quoted passage. Then make up a sentence which contains the word *horses'*.

3   Rewrite these passages with the *he said* (or its equivalent) moved forward to a position within the spoken part:

He said, 'I'm looking for a priest. You know what that means—a traitor to the republic.'

He said, 'Come nearer and let me have a good look at you.'

Someone shouted, 'Why do you want to know? Why are you asking so many questions?'

4   Improve the punctuation of this passage by changing one of the commas to a dash, another one to a colon, and another one to a full stop. Rewrite the passage in full, with the improvements put in:

The priest pushed the door open, it was the quiet hour of the early morning and the only sound was the cackling of the hens. He waited, wondering if it would be safe to go out into the square. Then suddenly, just as he was about to, he heard a sound that filled him with dread, the shriek of a whistle. He knew at once what it meant, the police had heard he was in the village and were coming to arrest him.

5   In the second paragraph, in order to speed up the narrative, Graham Greene merely quotes the lieutenant's questions, without telling us *who* he was questioning, or quoting any of the answers they gave. Make up a passage of dialogue in which three or four of the individuals who were questioned are identified. Quote the answers they gave. Let the lieutenant ask them the same questions that Graham Greene makes him ask. Identify the individuals only briefly (a beggar? . . . a cripple? . . . an old woman?), but introduce a few touches of descriptive detail about them if you want to. Before you begin look at the dialogue that comes a few lines lower down in the quoted passage, and notice that in this kind of dialogue the paragraphing alone is often enough to show which person is speaking.

35   Unnecessary words

There's no need to weigh up each word you write, in order to
see if you can leave it out because it's not contributing much
to the meaning. But it's not a good idea, either, to allow your
writing to become a clutter of *very*s and *really*s and *rather*s
and *absolutely*s and *somehow*s and *tend to*s and *of course*s.

Here are some different ways of writing sentences:

*I was completely and utterly bored. . . . I was bored.   This
tends to be quite a sad film. . . . This is a sad film.   She was
absolutely astonished. . . . She was astonished.   The
mountains were bathed in a very beautiful light. . . . The
mountains were bathed in a beautiful light.*

The lieutenant was examining something on the pommel of
his saddle: it seemed to be an old photograph. 'Let me see
your hands,' he said.

The priest held them up. They were as hard as a
labourer's. Suddenly the lieutenant leant down from the
saddle and sniffed at his breath. There was a complete silence
among the villagers—a dangerous silence, because it seemed
to convey to the lieutenant a fear. He stared back at the
hollow stubbled face and looked back at the photograph.

'All right,' he said, 'next.' And then, as the priest
stepped aside, 'Wait.' He put his hand down to the child's
head and gently tugged at her black stiff hair. He said,
'Look up. You know everyone in this village, don't you?'

'Yes,' she said.

'Who's that man, then? What's his name?'

'I don't know,' the child said.

The lieutenant caught his breath. 'Is he a stranger?'

Maria cried, 'Why, the child doesn't know her own
name. Ask her who her father is.'

'Who's your father?'

The child stared up at the lieutenant and then turned her
eyes upon the priest. The child said, 'That's him. There.'

'All right,' the lieutenant said. 'Next.' The
interrogations went on, while the sun came up above the
forest. The priest stood with his hands clasped in front of
him. Again death had been postponed.

---

1   Improve these sentences by leaving out some of the words. Make no other alterations. The number of words each sentence can be reduced to is given in brackets:

The police arrived so very suddenly that the priest had no time at all to hide anywhere. (13)

The village consisted of just about half a dozen huts or so, built of mud and wattle. (14)

The lieutenant's voice had a really bitter ring to it. (7)

There is no doubt whatsoever that this is an extremely exciting story. (5)

The characters in this novel tend to fall into two different categories. (9)

This is quite certainly one of the very best chapters in the whole of the book. (10)

2   Why is there a colon after the first sentence in the quoted passage?

3   Explain the meaning of the apostrophe in the word *child's* (line 11).

4   Make up a sentence which contains the word *child's*, but with the apostrophe having a different meaning.

5   Improve this passage. The writer has repeated nouns when he could have used pronouns, and he has mixed his tenses:

Suddenly the lieutenant jumped down from his horse and faced the priest directly. He glared at the priest for a few seconds. Then the lieutenant said, 'Let me see your hands.' The priest holds up his hands. His hands were as hard as a labourer's. The lieutenant then takes out the photograph again and examines it carefully. The priest could just see one corner of this photograph. The priest leant forward, trying to see what the photograph showed.

6   *The interrogations went on, while the sun came up above the forest.* Here Graham Greene gives us only the briefest glimpse of the countryside beyond the village, as it appeared at that moment. Can you fill out this glimpse of it by adding a few details? Try to visualise it, and describe it in two, three, or four sentences, which would form a continuation of the sentence we have quoted.

36 Padding

Padding is empty rubbish. Occasionally it may be there because the writer was trying to fill out a piece of writing that didn't look long enough. But usually it is not the result of a conscious purpose at all: it is there because the writer made no attempt to sort out what was worth saying from what was not.

It takes a very long time, several years in fact, to design and build a space rocket and equip it with all the latest modern devices that the scientists of today can think of, so that it is ready for launching into space.

How does the person who wrote that go about the task of writing? He puts everything down, however trivial or repetitive or obvious, the moment he thinks of it. A good writer goes about his task in the opposite way: he makes sure that everything he writes is worth saying.

The lieutenant said, 'Is no one willing to help? You heard what happened at Concepcion. I took a hostage there, and when I found that this priest had been in the neighbourhood I put the man against the nearest tree. . . . There's no need even to speak, if he's here among you. Just look at him. No one will know then that it was you who gave him away.'

The priest looked at the ground: he wasn't going to make it difficult for the man who gave him away.

'Right,' the lieutenant said, 'then I shall choose my man. You. You there. I'll take you.'

A woman screamed: 'That's my boy. That's Miguel. You can't take my boy.'

The priest stood silently. He could feel all round him the beginning of hate. He said, 'Lieutenant, I'm getting too old to be much good in the fields. Take me.'

'I'm choosing a hostage,' said the lieutenant, 'not offering free board and lodging to the lazy. If you are no good in the fields you are no good as a hostage.' He gave an order. 'Tie the man's hands and bring him along.'

---

1   Improve these passages by leaving out some of the words. Make no other alterations. The number of words each passage can be reduced to is given in brackets:

Graham Greene is generally considered by very many people to be one of the truly great and outstanding novelists of this present century. (14)

Brighton Rock *is the story of a boy called Pinkie, who becomes a teenage gang-leader, and he is the central character of the book. He has a very vicious and sadistic nature, a really cruel streak. He commits a whole series of absolutely ghastly crimes, carrying them out himself with his own hands, until he is hunted down and destroyed.* (38)

One of the most popular of all Graham Greene's novels is **The Third Man.** *It is not a serious novel and is altogether a rather light work, and in order to make this perfectly plain and clear to all and sundry he describes it as an 'Entertainment', showing that he does not regard it as being one of his important works.* (32)

It has to be said that these chapters are not very exciting and in a way even rather boring. (4)

2   Now reduce the passage given as an example on the opposite page (beginning *It takes a very long time . . .*) to 9 words.

3   Why is there a colon after the first sentence of the third paragraph of the extract?

4   Make up two sentences, about the lieutenant, or the priest, or Miguel, or Miguel's mother, and write them in such a way that you can put a colon after the first one.

5   In the last paragraph of the quoted passage Graham Greene does not describe the departure of the police in any detail. Try to picture it, and in a few sentences, which would form a continuation of his paragraph, describe them going off into the distance, towards the forest. But before you do this, read the description of their arrival, which comes in the last paragraph of the passage quoted on page 66, and in the first paragraph of the passage on page 68.

Acknowledgements

Grateful acknowledgement is made to the following for their kind permission to reprint copyright material:

Antonia Fraser: From *Mary, Queen of Scots*. Reprinted by permission of George Weidenfeld & Nicolson Ltd.

Graham Greene: From *The Power and the Glory*. Reprinted by permission of Laurence Pollinger Ltd. and William Heinemann Ltd. and The Bodley Head, publishers.

D. H. Lawrence: From *The Collected Short Stories of D. H. Lawrence*. Reprinted by permission of Laurence Pollinger Ltd., the Estate of the late Mrs. Frieda Lawrence Ravagli, and William Heinemann Ltd., publishers.

Daphne du Maurier: From *The Birds*. Reprinted by permission of Curtis Brown Ltd.